797,885 Books

are available to read at

Forgotten Books

www.ForgottenBooks.com

Forgotten Books' App
Available for mobile, tablet & eReader

ISBN 978-1-334-61473-6
PIBN 10734330

This book is a reproduction of an important historical work. Forgotten Books uses state-of-the-art technology to digitally reconstruct the work, preserving the original format whilst repairing imperfections present in the aged copy. In rare cases, an imperfection in the original, such as a blemish or missing page, may be replicated in our edition. We do, however, repair the vast majority of imperfections successfully; any imperfections that remain are intentionally left to preserve the state of such historical works.

Forgotten Books is a registered trademark of FB &c Ltd.
Copyright © 2017 FB &c Ltd.
FB &c Ltd, Dalton House, 60 Windsor Avenue, London, SW19 2RR.
Company number 08720141. Registered in England and Wales.

For support please visit www.forgottenbooks.com

1 MONTH OF FREE READING

at

www.ForgottenBooks.com

By purchasing this book you are eligible for one month membership to ForgottenBooks.com, giving you unlimited access to our entire collection of over 700,000 titles via our web site and mobile apps.

To claim your free month visit:
www.forgottenbooks.com/free734330

* Offer is valid for 45 days from date of purchase. Terms and conditions apply.

English
Français
Deutsche
Italiano
Español
Português

www.forgottenbooks.com

Mythology Photography **Fiction** Fishing Christianity **Art** Cooking Essays **Buddhism** Freemasonry Medicine **Biology** Music **Ancient Egypt** Evolution Carpentry Physics Dance Geology **Mathematics** Fitness Shakespeare **Folklore** Yoga Marketing **Confidence** Immortality Biographies Poetry **Psychology** Witchcraft Electronics Chemistry History **Law** Accounting **Philosophy** Anthropology Alchemy Drama Quantum Mechanics Atheism Sexual Health **Ancient History Entrepreneurship** Languages Sport Paleontology Needlework Islam **Metaphysics** Investment Archaeology Parenting Statistics Criminology **Motivational**

RECITED IN THE THEATRE, OXFORD,

JUNE VIII, MDCCCXLII.

OXFORD,
FRANCIS MACPHERSON.
1842.

RECITED IN THE THEATRE, OXFORD,

JUNE VIII, MDCCCXLII.

OXFORD,
FRANCIS MACPHERSON.
1842.

SYNOPSIS.

Charles in childhood—Charles after Pultowa—the contrast—The causes of the change—Scene on Pultowa the evening after the battle described—Flight into Turkey—Sees the last remnants of his army taken by the Russians as he crosses the frontier stream—Feelings at this crisis—Heroic manner in which he afterwards bears his fall—Sustained by hopes of the future and the remembrance of past glory—These remembrances described—including descent on Denmark—Narva—Passage of the Dwina—Field of Clissau on the morning of the battle, contrasted with its present aspect—The summit of his power—The Russian campaign—His overthrow as much the effect of the severe winter of 1705 as of the Czar's troops—His return to Sweden after long exile—Death before Frederickshall—Reflections.

[1] " In the palace of Stroemsholm there is a still finer picture whole length of Charles XII. in the ninth year of his age, leaning on a noble lion's head. Charles is here represented as a most beautiful boy: both his physiognomy and appearance are soft and effeminate, and (except in the lustre of his eye) by no means indicative of his subsequent character." Coxe's Travels in Scandinavia, vol. 3.

" There is in every human countenance either a prophecy or a history which must sadden or at least soften every reflecting observer." Coleridge's Literary Remains, vol. 1.

CHARLES THE TWELFTH.

Ἐν βιότου προτελείοις
Ἄμερον, εὐφιλόπαιδα,
Καὶ γεραροῖς ἐπίχαρτον.
. . .
Χρονισθεὶς δ' ἀπέδειξεν
Ἦθος τὸ πρὸς τοκήων.

Æschylus, Agamemnon, 720.

In that high dome [1], where Sweden's pictur'd kings,
Time-honor'd 'mid the unceasing change of things,
Chieftains and heroes—names of old renown—
Their day of warfare o'er, look calmly down,
Loveliest and noblest of his kingly race,
One child encircled with unfading grace
Brightens the air, around him and above,
With boyhood's golden light of peace and love.
Such radiant innocence, such cloudless mirth,
Dawn with the springtime o'er the laughing earth,
What time she calls from every green recess,
To wake the life of vernal loveliness.
Well may ye deem no shade of care or crime
Shall dim the sunshine of his morning prime,
Deem that this trance shall ne'er dissolve to show
How life's first vision hides a world of woe.

Would it were thus! O would that we might win
No other presage of the soul within!
But that bright eye hath glances too intense,
Too full, methinks, of storm and turbulence;
Behind the silence of those features lie
Unwakened thoughts, a voice, a prophecy:
The hour is nigh—yet *here*, thou Conqueror wild
Dream on for ever, be for aye a child!

Again I saw that face erewhile so fair,
So bright in boyhood—but a change was there;
A change of soul and aspect—many a storm
Had swept in anger o'er his manly form,
And darkened round his exile; childhood's gleam
Was now no more than a forgotten dream;
The prophecy fulfilled, a history now
Had traced its charact'ry on that stern brow:
Say whence this tale of woe? alas! too well
Thou dread Pultowa! it is thine to tell.

Lo! o'er thy battle plain another day,
In silence fleeting from the world away!
Another eve, and hush'd each living breath,
Mute Nature sorrowing o'er the field of death!
For through that silence on that lingering light
Full many a soul must wing its last long flight!
There on the cold earth 'neath the cold night sky
They sink together, foes with foes to die:
to aid, no voice of kindness near,
music on their d ear,

There in grim conflict with the unearthly Power
They wait the coming of the awful hour.
In that dread moment, when the pulse still beats
Faintly and feebly in " life's last retreats,"
Perchance the raven's[2] heavy-pinioned flight,
Darkly descending on the fall of night,
Startles some sleeper wildly from his dream,
Death's ghastly shadow; but so faint his scream,
His hand so nerveless may not scare away
The bird that waits not for a lifeless prey.

Yet think not of the dead—mourn not for them,
They are at rest, and ask no requiem;
But mourn for him, too sternly taught by fate
Earth was not made for man to desolate:
Queller of nations—the unconquered one—
Now crownless, realmless, homeless, all undone.
Yes, while the stars their pitying radiance shed,
O'er pale Pultowa and the slumbering dead,
Nightly they rose, the unpeopled desert o'er,
To guide his flight, who ne'er had fled before,
Till morn was breaking on the frontier steep,
Where Moslem sentinels their vigils keep.
Then o'er the waters to the royal Swede[3],
Weary and wounded on his path of speed,

[2] See Mazeppa, xviii.
[3] "It was some time before boats sufficient to transport the whole could be provided, by which accident five hundred Swedes and Cossacks fell into the hands of the enemy, who continued their pursuit quite to the banks of the river Bogh. This loss affected

There came a cry—the conqueror's savage boast—
O'er the poor remnants of his perished host.
He paused, he gazed upon that other shore,
Where suppliant ranks their chieftains aid implore,
And plead with all the eloquence that lies
In veteran looks and glorious memories;
In vain—the arm that taught the world to bow,
The unconquered arm—it hath no vengeance now.
And can he nought but weep? must bitter tears
Flow from the fountain that hath slept for years?
It was a rueful hour—what tongue may tell
The anguish of a warrior's last farewell?
The pang that wrung from that heroic eye
The tears of burning speechless agony?
Shame, grief, remorse, that pause concentered all,
The consummation of a mighty fall;
The dreary gathering in one hour of doom
Of all that's darkest on this side the tomb.

'Tis past—that brow is calm—no cloud is there,
The soul within has wrestled down despair.
Yes! he was kingly in his day of pride,
When erst from Warsaw waved his banners wide:
How doubly glorious now with front elate,
He stands unstooping in his hour of fate!

<small>the king more than all the former sufferings consequent on the defeat of Pultowa. He shed tears at seeing across the river the greater part of his few remaining friends carried away into captivity, without his having it in his power to offer them relief or assistance." Universal History, vol. 30.</small>

Aye, his the pride, the all-enduring will[4],
'Mid sternest suffering, how serenely still!
Others are drooping round him—his the mood
That will not yield, and cannot be subdued:
E'en now with light from memory's regions cast,
The future shines all glorious as the past,
And dreams and visions from the tented plain,
Come wildly gleaming o'er his soul again.

So, when the winds that raved the live-long night,
Have stilled their tumult with the dawning light,
So have I seen the cloud-rack fast and free,
Come thronging onward from the distant sea
Along the hill-tops, till the rising sheen
Of morn had spread their parted woof between,
And laughed away the masses dark and dull
Into a radiance glad and beautiful;
E'en thus the glorious past came floating by,
O'er the dark chambers of his memory;
Revealed before him in long line he saw
Denmark and Narva, Dwina and Clissaù,
Each with its throng of phantom hosts appears,
Bathed in the light of unforgotten years.

---

[4] "Une si facheuse situation, après le disastre que l'on venoit d'essuyer, répandoit la tristesse sur le visage d'en chacun. Il faut pourtant en excepter de roi; car ce Prince paroissoit toujours le même: nulle crainte apparente, nul changement dans son visage, et nulle plainte dans sa bouche." Puff. Hist. de Suede, vol. 3.

Again his father-land before him lay,
Bright with the dawning of his early day;
And long may Sweden, from her wave-worn steep,
Watch the morn kindling on the orient deep,
Ere such another o'er her hills and streams
Shall pour the promise of its rising beams.
Again the awakening voice of war is rolled
Onward from cliff to cliff, from hold to hold,
Till hill and plain with every peasant's home,
From southern headland to the northern foam,
Have heard the mustering trump proclaim to men
A new Gustavus is on earth again!
Once more he listened, while the morning gale
Whispered of triumph through his swelling sail;
Once more he kindles, while with eagle swoop
His banded hosts on cowering Denmark stoop,
And vows, as erst, amid the cannon's roar,
This shall my music be for evermore[5].

Then o'er him swept, as with a wing of flame,
All that awakes at Narva's deathless name,
And Dwina's flood before him rolled its wave,
Dark with the life-blood of the patriot brave.
There Poland's squadrons down the headlong steep
Strong as a whirlwind to the onset sweep,
There Stenau's lance and Courland's lordly plume[6]
Brighten the darkness of the battle gloom,

---

[5] "This henceforth shall be my music." See Voltaire.
[6] Mareschal Stenau and the Duke of Courland led the Poles.

While front to front with names of martial pride
Renschild and Holstein struggle side by side[7]
Amid the wavering van, that spent and foiled
Like broken billows from the shock recoiled.
"Onward for Sweden!" hark yon voice of might!
It stems, it turns the current of the fight,
'Mid thronging myriads the commanding form,
The cloud-compeller of the living storm;
'Tis Sweden's Hero, his the arm that wields
The doom of empires and the fate of fields.

An hundred years have rolled, since yonder sun[8]
Beheld a crown on Clissau lost and won.
There stood two nations in their war-array,
Two rival kings—but they have passed away.
And now when morn is dawning there serene,
The dew lies glistening, and the grass is green
Above a thousand graves.—How calm they rest,
The weary ones upon earth's quiet breast!
What tho' their sleep be all unwept and lone!
Nature round them a mother's arms has thrown,
And o'er their beds the skylarks soar and sing
Their morning carols thro' the early spring.

---

[7] Two of the Swedish Generals.————"They (the Swedes) gave way, were broken, and pursued even into the river. The King of Sweden rallied them in a moment, above his middle in water, as easily as if he had been exercising at a review." Voltaire.

[8] "The two Kings met on the 13th of July, in the year 1702, in a vast plain near Clissau, between Warsaw and Cracrow." Voltaire.

Yes! one deep quiet—one entire repose
Broods o'er that resting-place of friends and foes,
And the green hillocks, with their gentle swell,
Are all the record that remains to tell,
How Sweden triumphed, and how Poland fell.

From Clissau's field adown the golden west
The sun went hasting to his ocean rest;
But e'er he sank, one glance of glory came
To greet the Conqueror on his field of fame.
Strange that no boding, no prophetic fear
Foretold the sunset of his own career!
Yet why?—'mid fallen potentates he stood
Kingly, like Calpe, in his solitude,
And earth lay hushed around him: dark and vast
His shadow fell on many a nation cast;
It swept o'er humbled Denmark, eastward far
It flung its terror o'er the haughty Czar;
Behind him Poland low in ruin lay,
Before him Austria crouching in dismay!
And, England, e'en thy chief of proudest fame
Paused in the presence of a prouder name[9].

And O! if ere there burst o'er earth and sea
That thrilling sound—a nation's jubilee,

---

[9] See the account of Marlborough's visit to Charles at Altranstad, where he received embassies from almost all the Kings of Christendom. Voltaire, Trans. p. 98.

E'en then it woke in the triumphal song,
That rolled and revelled Sweden's hills along.
Ah! proud the pæan hymn—but fate hath thrown
O'er these high notes sad music all its own.
Lo! round the Invader's march the sullen mood
Of winter in his Scythian solitude,
With death and famine leagued!—doth Sweden's son
Deem these will own him as earth's kings have done?
Ah fated chief! e'en now their awful breath
Has chilled his legions with the blight of death:
Before him lies the desert, and behind
The sounds of vengeance deepen on the wind;
From Moscow's towers they come—a mighty throng—
As death insatiate, as the tempest strong.
Round Sweden's host is poured the banded might
Of Tartar wild, and hardy Muscovite;
Rings o'er the field of death their savage glee—
The work is done—the Invader where is he?

Fair the awakening, fair the blush of bloom,
When spring-time bursts on winter's months of gloom,
And loud with song and glad with sunlight thrills
Far through the dark woods and the silent hills.
Aye, fair the spring-time, but who hath not seen
More cloudless splendour, glory more serene
Cast on the earth!—how brightly, briefly cast!
When autumn paused in love to look its last,

Paused on the threshold of the western sky,
Lingering at sunset as though loth to die?
E'en such a gleam—so fleeting and so fair,
One moment lightened Sweden's long despair,
One moment woke his widow'd realms to sing
Strains of high welcome for their long-lost king;
How soon to cease! how soon shall tears be shed,
And requiems chanted for the warrior dead!

Athwart the vault of midnight deep and lone
The Arctic winter deeper gloom had thrown;
Night's heavenly warders, with unsleeping eye,
Kept watch along the battlements on high
Above the slumbering world, while darkness fell
On leaguring host and leagured citadel.
But *one* there slumbered not, *one* lawless will
Still dreamt of strife, tho' earth would fain be still,
Still dreamt of strife—but hush! he dreams no more—
There rung his knell, the life-long conflict o'er!
E'en like a wayward child with sleep opprest,
Sinking at day-fall on its mother's breast,
Earth's strongest son, her tempest-child of might
Lies hushed for ever in the arms of night.

O! ask not now if retribution just
Taught the proud Swede dominion is but dust—
If it was well that kings should learn, though late,
The hopes and fears of man to venerate.
O turn we rather from his wild career
     e with awe   on his silent bier

With the still night around—the stars above,
Those ancient teachers with their looks of love;
The self-same stars, that o'er man's troubled years
So long have shone from their eternal spheres:
Ages beneath have perished—they abide,
And night by night their stillness seems to chide
This changeful life—the ceaseless ebb and flow,
The weary turmoil of the world below.
Yea, these enduring heavens and this green earth—
That day by day since young creation's birth
With all their loving language never cease
To plead with man and call him back to peace,—
O teach they not that wars and tempests lie
Encompassed with a dread tranquillity,
That man's unquiet years of storm and strife
Are but as moments in the deeper life [10]
Of the Eternal Silence, on whose breast
All earthly discord sinks in perfect rest?

JOHN CAMPBELL SHAIRP,
BALLIOL COLLEGE.

[10] " Man's noisy years seem moments in the being
Of the eternal silence."
Wordsworth.